Kids en cuisine

KIDS EN CUISINE
RECIPE BOOK

Florence Rebattet

Published by New Generation Publishing in 2019

Copyright © Florence Rebattet 2019

First Edition

ISBN:
Paperback 978-1-78955-766-4
Hardback 978-1-78955-767-1

www.newgeneration-publishing.com

New Generation Publishing

How the story began...

I arrived in London in 2011, after having my son and for three years, I had the pleasure of spending special "mummy-son" time. Living in central London, I discovered so many children's activities, but, I also discovered that it could be very tricky to go out with a toddler in the rain or on public transport with the buggy, the special teddy, dummy, snacks and more, to reach an activity which lasted for thirty minutes. After so much effort to reach the class or activity, my little Edouard was either grumpy, hungry, didn't feel confident enough to join the fun, or even just fast asleep.

In 2013, there weren't many suppliers offering children's activities in the comfort of one's own home where kids could have a great afternoon with their friends and everyone, including the mums, could have a nice relaxing time in a friendly atmosphere. It was for this reason that I quit my "life in an office" as a Human Resource Manager and founded Kids En Cuisine.

I wanted to devote myself to my passions: children and cooking. I wanted to share my passion for healthy food by offering an activity which children could learn from, as well as enjoy. An added benefit was that it would also provide free time for the mums where they could enjoy a mummy chat without worrying if their children were bored or fighting over a toy. I wanted to share the joy that I had of cooking with my son with other children, teaching them how to cook from a very young age to gain skills which they could use for the rest of their lives.

It took me nine months to set up the business, come up with a name and create the recipes. In September 2014, on my thirty-first birthday, the story began with me providing private cooking classes in my clients' houses. Quite quickly I realised that I wanted to offer more than private sessions and I developed classes for birthday parties and then afternoon clubs in nurseries and schools. In the meantime, I also teamed up with some famous health food stores in London and developed monthly cooking classes so that many more children could discover the joys of healthy cooking.

After five years running Kids En Cuisine and often being asked for the recipes, I have decided to share the most popular recipes that I have created in this book. Each recipe has been taught to plenty of our little chefs and adapted to their special diets or tastes. That's why you will find a special little chef tip below every single recipe. I listened

to both the positive and negative feedback from the children and the parents, made changes to the recipes, and tried again and again until I found the right balance.

I have to confess that I was not a big fan of desserts but children love baking and it's nice to offer a mix of healthy cooking and baking classes over the term. Most of my dessert recipes have been designed for Ines and her mum, Nadine, who I have been visiting every Sunday morning for more than three years. They are big fans of chocolate, gluten-free healthy food. They push my boundaries a little bit further each week by asking me for new healthy baking recipes. Thanks to them, I had to leave my comfort zone and discovered that I really like baking, as long as I can make it healthy.

Another person who has always pushed my boundaries is my son. This little bundle of energy gave me the opportunity to develop my patience, my creativity, my daily food routine and my way of teaching calmly when I have to deal with fussy eaters and very active children. I have had to develop a lot of imagination and ways of mixing the flavours to feed Edouard. He is now eight years old and I am really proud when I see him in our kitchen making his breakfast (he's a big fan of French crepes!), his own tomato sauce or simply opening the fridge and the cupboards and trying to combine the ingredients to create his own recipes.

Kids

en cuisine

BREAKFAST

Hot chocolate with cocoa powder

Ingredients:

- 330ml of vegetable milk (coconut, almond, soya)
- 1 tablespoon of organic cocoa powder
- 1 teaspoon of honey or maple syrup

1. *Pour the vegetable milk into the blender.*
2. *Add the cocoa powder and the honey.*
3. *Blend for 20 seconds on high speed.*
4. *Warm the chocolate in a saucepan.*

Utensils:

* A blender
* A saucepan

Little chef tips:

Use vanilla almond milk to enjoy more flavour.

"I like using coconut milk for mine."

Preparation time: 5 minutes
Rest time: 1 hour
Cooking time: 10 minutes

French crepes

Ingredients for 8 crepes

- 40g of butter
- 120g of organic plain flour
- 2 organic eggs
- 250ml of organic skimmed-milk
- A pinch of salt
- Oil for the saucepan

Utensils:

* 2 mixing bowls
* A frying pan
* A whisk
* A scale

1. *Melt the butter using a "bain marie" (Alternatively place the butter in a small cooking glass container into a pan of hot water to melt slowly).*

2. *Pour the flour into a large mixing bowl and make a hole in the middle.*

3. *In the other mixing bowl, crack the eggs, gradually pour in the milk, add the salt, the melted butter and beat until smooth.*

4. *When all the ingredients are combined, pour the mixture into the flour and whisk until smooth.*

5. *Leave the mixture to rest for 30 minutes.*

6. *Preheat (medium heat) a lightly-oiled frying pan and pour a scoop of the crepe mixture into the saucepan. Loosen with a spatula, turn and cook the other side when it is nicely browned. Serve hot.*

Little chef tips:

If you want lighter crepes, you can add 150ml skimmed-milk and 100ml water.

For the toppings, feel free to add what you want: honey, brown sugar with lemon juice, jam for little chefs who like sweet crepes. Ham, olives or mozzarella for the ones who love salty crepes.

"I love mine with lemon and lime juice and coconut sugar. Try it!"

Preparation time: 10 minutes
Rest time: 30 minutes
Cooking time: 20 minutes

Pancakes

Ingredients for 10 pancakes

- 2 large eggs
- 150ml of skimmed milk
- 120g of organic plain flour
- 1 teaspoon of baking powder
- 3 tablespoons of granulated white sugar
- A pinch of salt
- Oil for the frying pan

Utensils:

* 2 bowls
* A frying pan
* An electric whisk
* A scale

1. *Crack the eggs and separate the yolk from the white. Put them in separate bowls.*

2. *In the bowl with the yolk, add the milk and stir.*

3. *Add the flour, a pinch of salt, the sugar and the baking powder. Whisk to a smooth batter.*

4. *In the bowl with the egg whites, whisk until you get "blanc en neige" (Whisk until stiff and forms soft peaks).*

5. *Add the egg whites to the mixture and leave it to rest for 30 min.*

6. *Prepare a medium frying pan, wipe it with some oiled kitchen paper and pour in a scoop of the mixture.*

7. *After 3 minutes (when your pancake begins to bubble), turn it over and cook until both sides are nicely brown. Serve hot.*

Little chef tips:

Add some maple syrup and blueberries on the top. Cook your pancake on a medium heat to avoid burning.

Preparation time: 5 minutes + 30 minutes rest
Cooking time: 5 minutes

Edouard's pancakes

Ingredients (12 pancakes):

- 100g of gluten free flour
- 250ml vanilla almond milk
- 50g of cinnamon sugar
- 1 tablespoon egg replacer
- 1 teaspoon of vanilla extract
- Oil for the pan

Utensils:

* A non-stick frying pan
* A spatula
* A large bowl
* A wooden spoon
* A scale

1. *In a large bowl, mix the flour, the sugar, the baking powder and the egg replacer.*

2. *Pour in the vanilla almond milk, the vanilla extract and mix until combined.*

3. *Let it rest for 30 minutes and then cook in a non-stick frying pan on a low heat. Flip it after 2/3 minutes and cook the other side.*

Little chef tips:

Crack 2 eggs if you don't have some egg replacer or use one tablespoon of apple puree.

"I made this recipe when we found out that Edouard had to follow a gluten-free diet for a few months."

Strawberry salad

Ingredients (2 servings)

- 250g of strawberries
- 2 kiwis
- 1 bunch of fresh mint
- ½ lemon
- 1 teaspoon of brown sugar

Utensils:

* A serving bowl
* A knife
* A chopping board

1. *Rinse and cut the strawberries into small pieces.*
2. *Peel and slice the kiwis.*
3. *Rinse the fresh mint leaves and cut them into tiny pieces.*
4. *Stir the strawberries, the kiwis and the mint together.*
5. *Squeeze the lemon and add the sugar.*

Little chef tips:

You can swap the mint with some basil leaves! Super yummy!
Use either a pair of scissors or your fingers to tear up the mint.
"*I like adding dry coconut on top of mine. Try it.*"

Preparation time: 5 minutes
Cooking time: 15 minutes
Rest time: 5 hours

Winter fruits salad

Ingredients (2 servings)

- 1kg of juicy oranges
- 100g of dried prunes
- 50g of dried apricots
- 2 cinnamon sticks
- 1 teaspoon of brown sugar

Utensils:

* A scale
* A knife
* A pan
* A frying pan

1. *Cut the oranges in half and squeeze out the juice.*
2. *Pour the juice into a hot frying pan and add the cinnamon sticks.*
3. *When it is boiling, add the dried apricots, prunes and turn off the cooker.*
4. *Cover and steam the mixture for 15 minutes.*
5. *Put it in the fridge. Eat when it is completely cool.*

Little chef tips:

If you do not have cinnamon sticks, use ground cinnamon (1 teaspoon).

"Sometimes, I add one apple cut into small pieces."

Roasted pineapple

Ingredients (2 servings)

- 1 large pineapple
- 2 teaspoons of cinnamon sugar
- Fresh raspberries

Utensils:

* A knife
* A chopping board
* Baking tray

1. *Preheat the oven to 200°C degrees.*
2. *With an adult's help, stand the pineapple upright and cut off the skin, following the curves.*
3. *Slice it and put it on a baking tray lined with greaseproof or baking paper.*
4. *Sprinkle with the cinnamon sugar (recipe given by the end of the book) and put it in the oven for 15 minutes.*
5. *When it is cooked, put the slices on a serving plate and add some fresh raspberries.*

Little chef tips:

You can swap the cinnamon sugar with fresh mint leaves and granulated sugar.

"I like using Victoria pineapple for this recipe"

Strawberry-banana smoothie

Ingredients for 1 glass (330ml)

- 200ml of almond milk
- 100ml of water (still or sparkling)
- 10 strawberries
- 1 banana
- 1 teaspoon of honey

Utensils:

* A blender
* A knife
* A glass

1. *Pour the almond milk and the water into the blender.*
2. *Rinse the strawberries and put them in with the banana.*
3. *Add the honey and blend all the ingredients together on a high setting for 1 minute.*

Little chef tips:

Add 2 tablespoons of strawberry or banana puree instead of the honey for a different texture.

"During the summer, I use frozen banana and strawberries."

Multivitamin smoothie

Ingredients for 2 glasses

- 6 oranges
- 3 blood oranges
- 1 mango
- 1 banana
- 10g of fresh ginger
- 200ml of vegetable milk (coconut, almond, oat, cashew)
- 100ml of coconut water

Utensils:

* A blender
* A knife
* A jar
* A scale

1. *Peel the oranges, mango, banana and ginger, cut into quarters, and put them in a blender.*
2. *Add the milk and the coconut water.*
3. *Blend on high until well mixed and add some ice cubes.*

Little chef tips:

You can use any kind of milk or fizzy water instead of coconut water.

Orange and lemon water

Ingredients for 1 glass (330ml each)

- ½ unwaxed orange
- ½ unwaxed blood orange
- ¼ unwaxed lemon
- 2 slices of fresh ginger
- 1l of water

Utensils:

* An empty water bottle
* A knife
* A jar

1. *Pour the water into the bottle.*
2. *Rinse the oranges and lemon before slicing them into small pieces.*
3. *Add them to the water and wait for 2 hours before drinking*

Little chef tips:

Vary this tasty water with any fruits or aromatic herbs you can find: strawberries, mint, lime, peaches, etc...

You can make it fizzy by using sparkling water.

"My favourite one is with 3 large slices of ginger, ½ unwaxed lemon, 7 mint leaves and 1 litre of water."

Kids
en cuisine

MAIN DISHES

Ratatouille

Ingredients (4 servings):

- 2 courgettes
- 1 aubergine
- 1 red and 1 yellow pepper
- 1kg of tomatoes
- 2 onions and 1 garlic clove
- Olive oil
- Basil leaves and thyme
- Salt and black pepper

Utensils:

* A peeler

* A saucepan

* A frying pan

* 6 small containers

* A chopping board

* A knife

* A tablespoon

1. *Boil 2 litres of water in a saucepan.*

2. *In the meantime, peel the vegetables and keep them in different containers. One for each vegetable.*

3. *When the water is boiling, make a cross at the bottom of the tomatoes and put them into the water for 3 minutes.*

4. *Drain and wait for 5 minutes before peeling the tomatoes with a knife.*

5. *Preheat a lightly-oiled frying pan and cook the courgette, aubergine, peppers, onion and garlic, separately. Your vegetables have to be cooked but still a little bit crunchy.*

6. *When all the vegetables are cooked, mix them in the frying pan with the tomatoes, the basil and the thyme. Cook all the ingredients for 5 minutes on a medium-low heat.*

Little chef tips:

To avoid the aubergine going brown, squeeze a lemon on it before cooking. Do not forget to add some salt on the vegetables before cooking them.

"I love having my ratatouille cold. It is very tasty and takes me back to Provence where I studied."

Preparation time: 15 minutes
Cooking time: 20 minutes

Chicken goujons

Ingredients (4 servings):

- 6 organic boneless and skinless chicken breasts
- 100g of plain flour
- 300g of breadcrumbs
- 2 large eggs or 3 small ones
- Salt and black pepper
- 1 tablespoon of olive oil

Utensils:

* A knife
* A chopping board
* A baking tray
* 3 shallow bowls
* A scale

1. *Preheat your oven to 180°C (160°C for a fan oven).*
2. *Crack the eggs and separate the yolks and the whites.*
3. *Pour the flour into a shallow bowl. Do the same with the breadcrumbs in another bowl.*
4. *Cut the chicken breasts into thin strips.*
5. *Roll the chicken in the flour, then in the beaten yolks and finally coat with the breadcrumbs.*
6. *Add some salt and black pepper.*
7. *Line a baking tray with baking paper and put the goujons in the oven for 20 minutes.*

Little chef tips:

To get more flavours, add some dry aromatic herbs or spices (oregano, basil, coriander, thyme, cumin, etc.) to the breadcrumbs or pour some truffle olive oil when it is cooked.

"I made this recipe for years when Edouard was little"

Preparation time: 15 minutes
Cooking time: 20 minutes

Salmon fish fingers

Ingredients (4 servings):

- 3 organic salmon fillets
- 100g of plain flour
- 400g of breadcrumbs
- 3 large eggs
- Salt and black pepper
- Olive oil
- Dill

Utensils:

* A knife + a fork
* A chopping board
* A baking tray
* 3 shallow bowls
* A scale

1. *Preheat your oven to 180°C (160°C for a fan oven).*

2. *Crack the eggs and separate the yolks and the whites.*

3. *Pour the flour into a shallow bowl. Do the same with the breadcrumbs in another bowl.*

4. *Cut the salmon into thin strips.*

5. *Roll the salmon strips in the flour, then in the beaten yolk and finally coat with the breadcrumbs.*

6. *Line a baking tray with baking paper and put it in the oven for 20 minutes.*

Little chef tips:

If you don't like salmon, you can use cod or any white fish.

Make it gluten free by using rice flour and gluten-free breadcrumbs.

"It is Edouard's favourite ones."

Vegan stuffed vegetables

Ingredients (4 servings):

- 2 courgettes
- 4 red peppers to fill
- 1 yellow + 1 red pepper
- 200g of brown rice
- ½ yellow onion
- 20g grated vegan mozzarella
- 1 garlic clove
- Olive oil
- Basil leaves
- Salt and black pepper

Utensils:

* A peeler
* A frying pan
* A knife
* A baking tray
* A shallow bowl
* A saucepan
* A strainer
* A scale
* A tablespoon

1. *Pre heat your oven to 200°C (180°C for a fan oven).*

2. *Boil 1 litre of water in the saucepan. When it's boiling, add the brown rice.*

3. *In the meantime, rinse the vegetables, peel the courgettes, the onion, the garlic clove and the yellow pepper. Chop them into small pieces and keep them in a shallow bowl.*

4. *Prepare the bell red peppers by removing the seeds and white insides.*

5. *When the rice is fully cooked, strain it and add it to the other ingredients. Stir.*

6. *Add salt, black pepper and basil leaves. Pour on some drops of olive oil.*

7. *Fill the red peppers by adding the rice mixture and bake in the oven for 30 minutes.*

Little chef tips:

Add some tiny pieces of tofu to get a "cheesy" texture.

"I eat my vegan stuffed pepper raw: as a sandwich for picnic"

Preparation time: 15 minutes
Cooking time: 45 minutes

Vegan
Gluten Free

Courgette and sweet potato crumble

Ingredients (4 servings):

- 2 courgettes
- 1 sweet potato
- 1 yellow onion
- Herbs de Provence
- Crumble (Recipe at the end of the book)
- Salt and black pepper
- Olive oil

Utensils:

* A knife
* A chopping board
* A baking dish

1. *Preheat your oven to 180°C (160°C for a fan oven).*
2. *Peel the courgettes, the sweet potato and slice into small pieces.*
3. *Put them in a greased baking dish and sprinkle on some herbs de Provence, salt and black pepper.*
4. *Cover with the crumble.*
5. *Put it in the oven for 45 minutes.*

Little chef tips:

The thinner your courgettes and sweet potato are, the better it tastes and the cooking time will be faster.

Preparation time: 15 minutes
Cooking time: 15 minutes

Croque Monsieur

Ingredients (4 servings):

- 8 pain de mie (soft bread) slices
- 50g of butter
- 200ml of béchamel sauce
- 100g of cheddar cheese
- 8 cooked ham slices (2 slices per croque monsieur)
- Salt and black pepper

Utensils:

* A knife
* A baking tray
* A scale
* A tablespoon

1. *Preheat your oven to 180°C (160°C for a fan oven) and line a baking tray with baking paper.*
2. *Spread some butter on one side of the pain de mie and put it on the baking tray. Repeat the action 3 times to get 4 croque monsieur.*
3. *Add some grated cheddar, then the ham slices, then 1 tablespoon of béchamel sauce.*
4. *Finish your croque monsieur with a pain de mie slice and add some béchamel sauce on the top with salt and black pepper.*
5. *Put them in the oven for 15 minutes to melt the cheese.*

Little chef tips:

If you don't like béchamel sauce, swap it for mozzarella and basil leaves.

Preparation time: 20 minutes
Cooking time: 15 minutes

Rainbow pizza

Ingredients (1 pizza):

- 1 pizza dough
- 30g of sweetcorn
- 1 orange pepper
- 1 red pepper
- 1 courgette
- 1 aubergine
- 200g of black olives
- 150ml of tomato sauce

Utensils:

* A knife
* A chopping board
* A baking tray
* A rolling pin
* 5 small cups/bowls
* 1 tablespoon
* A scale

1. *Preheat your oven to 220°C (200°C for a fan oven).*
2. *Use your rolling pin to spread the pizza dough and make a circle.*
3. *Chop all the vegetables into small pieces and keep them in separate bowls.*
4. *Spread the tomato sauce onto the pizza dough by using the back of the spoon.*
5. *Think about the rainbow colours and arrange the ingredients in the right way and in a circle.*
6. *Put your pizza in the oven for 15 minutes.*

Little chef tips:

You can use the same ingredients and make a caterpillar pizza instead of a rainbow pizza.

Preparation time: 15 minutes
Cooking time: 20 minutes

Carrot and cumin mini-cakes

Ingredients (4 servings):

- 2 carrots
- 100g of grated mozzarella
- 1 tablespoon of cumin
- 2 eggs
- 200g of flour
- 10cl of milk
- 10cl of olive oil
- 1 tablespoon of baking powder

Utensils:

* A knife
* A chopping board
* Mini cake moulds
* A peeler
* A grater
* A scale
* A wooden spoon

1. *Preheat your oven to 180°C (160°C for a fan oven).*
2. *Peel and grate the carrots. Keep them on a plate for later.*
3. *In the bowl, add the flour, crack the eggs and stir.*
4. *Add the milk, the olive oil and the cheese. Mix them together.*
5. *When the mixture is smooth, add the cumin, salt, black pepper and the baking powder.*
6. *Pour the mixture into the moulds and put them in the oven.*

Little chef tips:

It's delicious when you add some black olives and cooked ham.

You can choose any cheese you like.

"Edouard loved this recipe when he was two years old."

Preparation time: 15 minutes
Cooking time: 30 minutes

Provencal tart

Ingredients for the filling (4 servings):

- 1 courgette
- 1 aubergine
- 3 tomatoes
- 1 yellow pepper
- 150ml of tomato sauce
- Basil leaves and olive oil

Utensils:

* A knife
* A chopping board
* A pie mould
* A frying pan
* A scale
* A wooden spoon

Ingredients for the pastry:

- 200g of organic plain flour
- 120g of soft butter, cut into pieces
- 1 teaspoon of salt
- 1 teaspoon of olive oil and 80ml of water

1. *Preheat your oven to 180°C (160°C for a fan oven). Line the pie mould with greaseproof paper, roll out the pastry to a circle and cook it for 15 minutes.*

2. *While the pastry is cooking, peel the courgette and chop it into small pieces.*

3. *Cut the aubergine, peppers, tomatoes and basil leaves. Fry all the vegetables together with some olive oil. When they're cooked, pour in the tomato sauce and cook for 5 minutes.*

4. *Fill your cooked pastry with the vegetables, then chop the basil leaves and put them on the top.*

Little chef tips:

You can add some grated cheese (mozzarella) and put it in the oven for 5 minutes to melt it.

"One of my favourite dishes".

Preparation time: 15 minutes
Cooking time: 20 minutes + 20 minutes

Quiche Lorraine

Ingredients for the filling (4 servings):

- 300ml of double cream
- 1 egg
- 250g of pancetta cubes/lardons
- 200g of grated Emmental cheese
- Salt and black pepper

Utensils:

* A bowl
* A pie mould
* A wooden spoon
* A scale

Ingredients for the pastry:

- 200g of organic plain flour
- 120g of soft butter, cut into pieces
- 1 teaspoon of salt
- 1 teaspoon of olive oil
- 80ml of water

1. *Preheat your oven to 180°C (160°C for a fan oven).*
2. *Line the pie mould with greaseproof paper, roll out the pastry into a circle and cook it for 20 minutes (the method is in the 'Basics' chapter).*
3. *While the pastry is cooking, pour the double cream and the milk into a bowl and stir.*
4. *Crack the eggs and add them to the quiche mixture with the grated cheese. Mix well until you can't see the yolk any more.*
5. *Add the pancetta cubes and pour the mixture into the cooked pastry.*
6. *Put it back in the oven for 20 minutes.*

Little chef tips:

Use mozzarella if you do not have Emmental cheese.

Quinoa corn muffins

Ingredients (8 muffins):

- 200g of polenta
- 100g of cornflour
- 1 tablespoon of baking powder
- 140g of cooked quinoa
- 250ml of vegetable milk (almond, coconut, oat, cashew)
- 3 medium eggs
- 4 teaspoons of coconut oil
- Coriander and salt
- Pumpkin and chia seeds

Utensils:

* A 12-hole muffin tray
* 1 big and 1 small bowl
* A wooden spoon
* A whisk
* A scale

1. *Preheat the oven at 200°C.*
2. *In a large bowl, mix the dry ingredients together. Then add the cooked quinoa. Stir well.*
3. *In the small bowl, pour the vegetable milk, crack the eggs and whisk.*
4. *In the large bowl, combine the dry and the wet ingredients together, then add the chopped coriander and pumpkin seeds.*
5. *Fill the muffin tray and put it in the oven.*

Little chef tips:

These muffins are perfect when you dip them into hummus or tapenade.

Pea soup

Ingredients (4 servings):

- 500g of frozen or fresh peas
- 200ml of oat cream
- 10 mint leaves
- 10 basil leaves
- 20 coriander leaves
- Salt and black pepper

Utensils:

* A blender
* A saucepan
* A wooden spoon
* A scale

1. *Simmer the peas in boiling water for 4 minutes and drain.*
2. *Use the blender and pour all the ingredients in it.*
3. *Blend until you get a velvety texture (2 minutes high power).*

Little chef tips:

Pour in some water to get a liquid texture.

"Sometimes I use coconut milk instead of oat milk and I squeeze one lime"

Quinoa and bulgur salad

Ingredients (4 servings):

- 200g of white quinoa
- 200g of bulgur
- 1 lime
- 500g of tomatoes
- ½ yellow pepper
- ½ red onion
- 1 garlic clove
- Fresh mint and coriander leaves
- Salt and black pepper

Utensils:

* A knife
* A chopping board
* A pan
* A strainer
* A bowl

1. *Rinse the quinoa and the bulgur in fresh water. Then, put them in a pan with cold water and let them cook for 10 minutes.*

2. *In the meantime, dice the pepper, red onion, tomatoes and the garlic.*

3. *When the quinoa and bulgur are cooked, drain them.*

4. *In a bowl, mix all the ingredients together and squeeze in the lime.*

5. *Add the basil, coriander, salt and the black pepper. Put your salad in the fridge for 1 hour before eating it.*

Little chef tips:

If you don't like crunchy quinoa, cook it in another saucepan for 15 minutes, drain it and then mix it with the bulgur.

"This recipe became one of my basics for years for our family meals"

Greek salad

Ingredients (4 servings):

- 1 large cucumber
- 200g of feta
- 100g of black olives
- 2 large tomatoes
- ½ green and red pepper
- 1 red onion
- ½ lemon juice
- 2 tablespoons of olive oil
- Salt and black pepper
- Dried oregano

Utensils:

* A knife
* A chopping board
* A bowl
* A scale
* A peeler

1. *Peel the cucumber and chop it into small pieces.*
2. *Slice the tomatoes, peppers and the red onion and add them to the cucumber.*
3. *Cut the feta into cubes add it to the bowl and sprinkle in some salt, black pepper and dried oregano.*
4. *Squeeze the lemon and pour in the olive oil.*

Little chef tips:

You can find feta cheese already cut into small pieces.

"Sometimes, I add some dried tomatoes and dried goat cheese"

Gluten-free pasta salad

Ingredients (4 servings):

- 200g of coral lentil pasta
- 200g of gluten-free pasta
- 1 yellow pepper + 1 red
- ½ red onion
- 1 can of sweetcorn
- 2 spring onions
- ½ lemon juice
- 4 slices of organic smoked salmon
- 3 tablespoons of olive oil + 1 tablespoon of balsamic vinegar
- Salt, black pepper and basil leaves

Utensils:

* A knife
* A chopping board
* A bowl
* 2 saucepans
* A scale
* A wooden spoon

1. *Boil water in two saucepans. Cook your gluten-free pasta in one and the coral lentil pasta in the other.*
2. *In the meantime, dice the spring onions and the peppers and put them in your serving bowl.*
3. *Drain and rinse the sweetcorn and mix it with the peppers and spring onions.*
4. *Slice the smoked salmon into thin pieces and squeeze ½ the lemon on it. Add it to the vegetables.*
5. *When your pastas are cooked, drain, let them cool down and add them to the other ingredients.*
6. *Make your dressing with the olive oil, balsamic vinegar, salt, black pepper and basil leaves. Pour it on the salad!*

Little chef tips:

If you don't have time to cool down the pasta, rinse with cold water.

Carrot and orange salad

Ingredients (4 servings):

- 700g of organic carrots
- 1 orange
- 1 lemon
- Basil leaves
- Fresh coriander
- Salt and black pepper

Utensils:

* A scale
* A knife
* A grater
* A peeler
* A pair of scissors

1. *Peel your carrots. Remember to ask an adult to help you if you are not confident with a peeler.*

2. *Grate your carrots as thin as you can.*

3. *With a knife, peel the orange and cut it into small pieces and add to the carrots.*

4. *Cut the lemon in half and squeeze it on the carrots.*

5. *Snip the basil and coriander leaves with your scissors and sprinkle on some salt and black pepper.*

Little chef tips:

If you don't like lemon, pour some drops of olive oil.

"I like adding some cashew nuts, black sesame seeds and sunflower seeds for mine"

Fennel salad

Ingredients (4 servings):

- 1 fennel bulb
- ½ pomegranate
- Mint leaves
- Salt and black pepper
- 2 tablespoons of olive oil
- 1 teaspoon of raspberry vinegar

Utensils:

* A knife
* A chopping board
* A serving bowl
* A tablespoon

1. *Wash the fennel bulb with tap water.*
2. *Separate the leaves from the stem.*
3. *Chop the fennel into really small pieces and put it in a serving bowl.*
4. *Slice your pomegranate in half and separate the seeds from the white parts.*
5. *Add them to the fennel.*
6. *Rip up the mint leaves, then add salt and black pepper.*
7. *Pour on some the olive oil, the raspberry vinegar and stir.*

Little chef tips:

If it's too hard for your little chef's hands to take out the seeds from the pomegranate, you can buy some that have already been cleaned in the supermarket.

"One of my first recipes when I started Kids En Cuisine"

Lentil salad

Ingredients (4 servings):

- 200g of Puy lentils
- 2 chicken breast fillets
- 1 yellow onion
- 6 radishes
- ½ orange pepper
- 20g cashew nuts
- 1 avocado
- Herbs de Provence, salt and black pepper
- 3 tablespoons of olive oil + 1 tablespoon of balsamic vinegar
- 1 teaspoon of Dijon mustard

Utensils:

* A knife
* A chopping board
* A frying pan
* A saucepan
* A serving bowl
* A cup for the dressing
* A spoon

1. *Rinse your Puy lentils under the water before cooking them (20 minutes) in 1.5 litres of boiling water.*

2. *In the frying pan, cook the chicken breasts with some oil and salt. When it is cooked, cut them into small pieces and put them in the serving bowl.*

3. *Add the lentils after draining them.*

4. *Chop the yellow onion, the orange pepper, and the skinned avocado into small pieces. Sprinkle some herbs de Provence, salt and black pepper on top of your salad.*

5. *Make the dressing with the olive oil, balsamic vinegar and Dijon mustard.Leave in the fridge for an hour before eating.*

Little chef tips:

You can use green or black lentils if you do not find Puy lentils.

It will be tasty too.

"Each time, I cook some lentils, I always think about the traditional French dish from Toulouse, my city: Saucisse-lentille"

Bruschetta

Ingredients (2 servings):

- 2 ciabatta slices
- 3 tomatoes
- 1 yellow onion
- 1 mozzarella Di Bufala
- 1 garlic clove
- 5 basil leaves
- Salt and black pepper
- 1 tablespoon of olive oil

Utensils:

*A knife

* A chopping board

*A bowl

* A spoon

1. *Toast the ciabatta slices and rub the garlic clove on them. (Let them cool down before rubbing the garlic.)*

2. *Cut the tomatoes into small cubes and take out the seeds.*

3. *Slice the onion and the mozzarella into small pieces and add them to the tomatoes.*

4. *Rip up the basil leaves, sprinkle on some salt, black pepper and pour on some olive oil.*

5. *Stir and put the tomato mixture on the bread.*

Little chef tips:

If the flavour of the buffalo mozzarella is too strong, you can use a normal mozzarella one.

If you can't find a ciabatta, you can use a baguette.

"For mine: I use brown toasted bread with a lot of garlic and some pumpkin seeds on the top!"

Non-fried vegetable rolls

Ingredients (4 servings):

- 16 rice sheets
- 2 carrots
- 1 cucumber
- 1 red pepper
- Mint leaves
- 50g rice noodles

Utensils:

* A knife
* A chopping board
* A bowl
* A serving platter
* A saucepan

1. *Cook the rice noodles for 3 minutes in boiling water then drain.*
2. *Chop the cucumber, pepper and carrots into long, thin sticks.*
3. *Dip the rice sheets into lukewarm water until they are soft. Put the wet rice sheet on the table, add the rice noodles, the vegetable sticks, put the mint leaves on the top and roll.*

Little chef tips:

Think about taking out the seeds from the cucumber to avoid too much water.

You can dip your vegetable rolls in soya sauce.

DESSERTS

Preparation time: 20 minutes
Rest time: 2 hours

Kids En Cuisine's tiramisu

Ingredients (2 servings):

- 100g of double cream
- 100g of mascarpone
- 30g of coconut sugar
- 4 large strawberries
- 1 teaspoon of vanilla extract
- 1 mug of hot chocolate
- Cocoa powder
- 20 boudoir biscuits

Utensils:

* A knife
* A chopping board
* A large bowl
* A whisk
* A tablespoon
* A scale

1. *In the large bowl, whisk the double cream and the mascarpone until they have completely mixed and have the consistency of thickly whipped cream.*

2. *Add the vanilla extract and coconut sugar. Mix well.*

3. *Dip the boudoir biscuits into the hot chocolate until soaked but not soggy.*

4. *Layer your serving plate with the soaked biscuits then spread over the creamy mixture. Repeat twice.*

5. *Finish your tiramisu with the creamy layer and add some chopped strawberries on the top.*

6. *Sprinkle some cocoa powder and put in the fridge for a few hours.*

Little chef tips:

You can use any biscuits or sponge fingers that you like. But please note that for an authentic tiramisu, use a mug of coffee instead of hot chocolate.

Preparation time: 15 minutes
Cooking time: 12 minutes

Coconut balls

Ingredients (6 balls):

- 150g of grated coconut
- 1 egg
- 5g soft butter (optional)
- 40g golden sugar

Utensils:

* A large bowl

* A scale

* A whisk

* A wooden spoon

1. *Crack the egg in the bowl, whisk until you get some bubbles on the top.*
2. *Add the sugar and whisk until smooth.*
3. *Poor on the grated coconut and stir with a wooden spoon.*
4. *Add the soft butter and combine it with the mix by using your fingers.*
5. *Make nice and compact coconut balls by squeezing them very well.*
6. *Line a baking tray and put them in the oven for 12 minutes at 200°C.*

Little chef tips:

If you don't make compact coconut balls, it will be tricky to cook them. You can use a muffins tray to cook them and keep nice and tidy coconut balls.

"I like adding a teaspoon of vanilla paste on mine"

Preparation time: 20 minutes
Cooking time: 1 hour

Meringues

Ingredients (15 meringues):

- 3 eggs
- 110g of granulated white sugar

Utensils:

* Large bowl
* Electric whisker
* A baking tray
* A scale
* An icing bag

1. *Crack the eggs and separate the yolks from the whites.*
2. *Put the egg whites in a large bowl.*
3. *Take the electric whisker, put it on the medium speed and whisk.*
4. *Add the sugar gradually, whisking all the time.*
5. *Line a baking tray, fill an icing bag with the meringue mix and make nice and bumpy circles.*
6. *Put them in the oven at 120°C for 1 hour.*

Little chef tips:

If you want crunchy meringues outside but really soft inside, cook them for only 40 minutes.

"Edouard loves his meringues when they are small and crunchy. He started making his own ones when he was only four years old and he is still addicted to them. Especially when he is back from school"

Preparation time: 20 minutes
Cooking time: 15 minutes

Kids En Cuisine's biscuits

Ingredients (12 biscuits):

- 120g of soft butter
- 280g of plain flour
- 150g of granulated white sugar
- 1 teaspoon of orange extract
- 1 egg
- 1 yolk egg

Utensils:

* A large bowl
* A rolling pin
* Cookie cutters
* A pastry brush
* A scale

1. *In a large bowl, mix the dry ingredients (sugar and flour) with your hands.*

2. *Add the soft butter to the mix and crack the egg. Mix with your hands until you get a nice dough.*

3. *Add the orange extract and knead the dough.*

4. *With a rolling pin, flatten the dough (2cm thick) and use your cookie cutters to get the shapes that you want.*

5. *Line a baking tray and put your biscuits on it. Before putting them in the oven, use a yolk and brush your biscuits with it to get a nice golden colour.*

Little chef tips:

If your dough is too sticky or sticks on the rolling pin, use some flour like dust.

Preparation time: 15 minutes
Cooking time: 12 minutes

Kids En Cuisine's cookies

Ingredients (12 cookies):

- 150g of plain flour

- 50g of cinnamon sugar

- 1 teaspoon of honey

- 100g of dark chocolate chips

- 20g of soft unsalted butter

- 1 teaspoon of baking powder

- 1 teaspoon of cacao powder

- 1 medium egg

- 2 teaspoons of bee pollen

Utensils:

* 2 large bowls

* A wooden spoon

* A baking tray

* A scale

1. *In a bowl, combine the dry ingredients: flour, cinnamon sugar, chocolate chips, bee pollen, baking powder and cacao powder.*

2. *In a separate bowl, crack the egg and whisk. Then, combine it with the honey.   Pour the mix into the dry ingredients and stir with a wooden spoon.*

3. *Add the soft butter and knead the mixture until you get a nice dough.*

4. *Line a baking tray, make some balls (the size of your hands) and flatten them (nicely) on the tray.*

5. *Put them in the oven for 15 minutes at 200°C.*

Little chef tips:

Use some flour as dust if it's too sticky. If you don't like honey, swap

it for some maple syrup.

"I like using salted butter for mine"

Preparation time: 15 minutes
Cooking time: 45 minutes

Flo's cooked apples

Ingredients (4 servings):

- 4 big red apples
- 2 tablespoons of cinnamon sugar
- 1 lemon
- 20cl water

Utensils:

* A baking tray
* A knife

1. *Clean the apples under cold running water.*
2. *Put them on the baking tray, sprinkle the cinnamon sugar on top.*
3. *Squeeze the lemon and pour the juice over the apples.*
4. *Add 20cl water in the baking tray and put it in the oven for 45 minutes at 220°C. Your apples will be cooked soft.*

Little chef tips:

Change the flavours by swapping the cinnamon sugar with vanilla sugar.

You can also add a teaspoon of orange extract to the lemon juice.

"Love this simple dessert during Winter time with a glass of hot vanilla almond milk"

Preparation time: 20 minutes
Cooking time: 20 minutes

Frangipane

Ingredients (4 serves):

- 2 sheets of puff pastry
- 70g of ground almonds
- 100g granulated white sugar
- 50g of soft unsalted butter
- 2 medium eggs
- 1 egg yolk
- 1 teaspoon of almond extract

Utensils:

* A baking tray
* A knife
* A large bowl
* A wooden spoon
* A pastry brush
* A scale

1. *Unroll your puff pastry and make a circle. Use a serving plate to get a nice large circle.*

2. *In the large bowl, mix the ground almonds, the sugar, the eggs and the soft butter to make the frangipane mix.*

3. *Combine the ingredients and mix until you get a smooth, thick texture.*

4. *Add the frangipane mix to the middle of the puff pastry and spread it with the back of a spoon. Be sure that you leave a space of 1 cm without the mix around the edge of the pastry.*

5. *Add the other puff pastry sheet to the top and squeeze all around it to attach it to the one on the bottom.*

6. *With a knife, draw some nice lines and brush them with the egg yolk.*

7. *Put it in the oven at 200°C for 20 minutes.*

Little chef tips:

Use a knife to make some drawings on the top.

Preparation time: 20 minutes
Cooking time: 30 minutes

Rose pies

Ingredients (4 serves):

- 1 puff pastry sheet
- 2 red apples
- ½ lemon
- Raspberry jam
- 1 tablespoon of beetroot juice
- 250ml still water

Utensils:

* A 4 hole muffin tray
* A knife or mandolin
* A large bowl
* A wooden spoon

1. *Core the apples and cut them in half. Slice them really thinly with a sharp knife. If you have a mandolin, use it very carefully.*

2. *Put the apple slices in a large bowl, add the lemon juice and the beetroot juice and soak them in 250ml water.*

3. *Microwave the bowl for 30 seconds at the maximum power. Your apple slices should be very soft and pliable.*

4. *Divide your puff pastry sheet into 4 straight lines. Spread some raspberry jam all over.*

5. *Arrange the apple slices and overlap one another to create a line on the top. We have to see 2cm of the apple over the puff pastry.*

6. *Fold the bottom of the puff pastry and cover your apple slices.*

7. *Roll gently and put your rose pie in the muffin tray. Put them in the oven at 220°C for 30 minutes.*

Little chef tips:

Sprinkle some brown sugar on the top before putting your rose pies in the oven.

Preparation time: 20 minutes
Cooking time: 15 minutes

Madeleines

Ingredients (20 madeleines):

- 120g of plain flour
- 120g of granulated white sugar
- 120g unsalted butter
- 3 medium eggs
- Zest of one unwaxed lemon
- 1 lemon
- 1 teaspoon of baking powder

Utensils:

* A madeleine tray
* 2 bowls
* A wooden spoon
* A grater
* A scale
* A saucepan

1. *In a large bowl, mix the flour, the sugar and the baking powder.*

2. *Crack the eggs and separate the yolks from the whites. The yolk goes with the dry ingredients and the whites in a separate bowl.*

3. *Whisk the white with a fork until you get bubbles on the top. Add them to the mix and combine.*

4. *Melt the butter, in a saucepan, and wait until it cools down before pouring it on the mix.*

5. *Add the lemon juice and the zest. Stir well.*

6. *Pour in the madeleine moulds and put them in the oven at 240°C for 6 minutes and then 180°C for 8 minutes. Your madeleines are ready when you see a little mountain on the top and a nice golden colour.*

Little chef tips:

Swap the lemon for ½ an orange or rose water.

"I really like mine with rose water and dry pieces of rose in the dough!"

Preparation time: 20 minutes
Cooking time: 15 minutes

Chocolate and courgette muffins

Ingredients (12 muffins):

- 200g of dark chocolate (70%)
- 50g of coconut sugar
- 60g of plain flour
- 150g grated courgette
- 3 medium eggs
- 1 teaspoon of baking powde

Utensils:

* A 12 hole muffin tray
* A scale
* A large bowl
* A wooden spoon
* A saucepan

1. *Crack the eggs and whisk until you get some bubbles. Add the coconut sugar and mix well until smooth.*
2. *Melt the chocolate in a saucepan and let it cool down on the side.*
3. *Grate the courgette and add it to the mixture.*
4. *Pour the melted chocolate, mix it, add the flour and the baking powder.*
5. *Pour the mixture into the muffin tray and put it in the oven at 220°C for 15 minutes.*

Little chef tips:

The flour could be optional. If you don't add it, cook the mixture for 10 more minutes.

"There are always some muffins in my freezer ready to be warm and eat at any time"

Chocolate courgette and sweet potato muffins

Ingredients (12 muffins):

- 200g of dark chocolate (70%)
- 50g of coconut sugar (optional)
- 200g of cooked sweet potatoes
- 150g of grated courgette
- 1 teaspoon of gluten-free baking powder

Utensils:

* A 12 hole muffin tray
* A scale
* A large bowl
* A wooden spoon
* A blender

1. *Melt the chocolate, in a saucepan, and let it cool down on the side.*

2. *In a blender, add the sweet potatoes, the sugar, the grated courgette and the chocolate. Blend until you get a smooth texture.*

3. *Add the baking powder and blend again.*

4. *Pour the mixture into the muffin tray and put it in the oven at 200°C for 20 minutes.*

Little chef tips:

To get more moisture and keep the cake vegan and gluten free, add 100g of soft tofu and cook it for 10 more minutes. Before eating it, wait until it is completely cold as the texture won't be nice with hot tofu.

Preparation time: 15 minutes
Cooking time: 20 minutes

Chocolate and beetroot muffins

Ingredients (12 muffins):

- 200g of dark chocolate (70%)
- 40g of coconut sugar
- 80g of plain flour
- 200g raw beetroot
- 2 large eggs
- 1 teaspoon of baking powder

Utensils:

* A 12 hole muffin tray
* A scale
* A large bowl
* A wooden spoon
* A peeler
* A saucepan

1. *Crack the eggs and whisk until you get some bubbles. Add the coconut sugar and mix well until smooth.*

2. *Melt the chocolate, in a saucepan, and let it cool down on the side.*

3. *Peel the beetroot, grate it and add it to the mixture.*

4. *Pour the melted chocolate in, mix it, add the flour and the baking powder. Pour the mixture into the muffin tray and put it in the oven at 220°C for 15 minutes.*

Little chef tips:

You can use 90g of granulated white sugar instead of coconut sugar.

Preparation time: 20 minutes
Cooking time: 20 minutes

Lemon and chia seeds cakes

Ingredients (6 muffins):

- 100g of plain flour
- 120g of dark chocolate (70%)
- 80g of coconut sugar
- 80g of unsalted butter
- ½ lemon + zest
- 1 tablespoon of chia seeds
- ½ tablespoon of baking powder
- 2 eggs

Utensils:

* A wooden spoon
* A 6-hole muffin tray
* A scale
* 2 large bowls

1. *Melt the butter and let it cool down on the side.*

2. *In a large bowl, mix the butter, the eggs and the flour.*

3. *In a separate bowl, combine the eggs and the sugar until the mix is slightly white with bubbles on the top. Then, pour the flour into the mixture and stir.*

4. *Squeeze the lemon and add the zest.*

5. *Add the chia seeds and the baking powder. Stir until you combine all the ingredients together.*

6. *Pour the mixture into the muffin tray and put it in the oven at 220°C for 15 minutes.*

Little chef tips:

You can swap the chia seeds with poppy seeds for a different flavour.

"One of my first sweet recipes when I started Kids En Cuisine"

Preparation time: 20 minutes
Cooking time: 15 minutes

Strawberry crumble

Ingredients (1 small crumble):

- 200g of fresh strawberries
- 1 tablespoon of coconut sugar
- 1 lemon
- 8–10 mint leaves

Utensils:

* 1 small oven tray
* A chopping board
* A knife
* A scale

1. *Wash the strawberries under running water.*
2. *Take the leaves off the strawberries and cut into quarters and put them on the tray.*
3. *Rip the mint leaves with your fingers and add them to the strawberries.*
4. *Squeeze a lemon over the strawberries and sprinkle over the sugar.*
5. *Cover the strawberries with the crumble mix*
6. *Put in the oven at 180°C for 30 minutes.*

Little chef tips:

Use any fruits you want and create your own special crumble.

BASICS

Guacamole

Ingredients (4 servings):

- 2 avocados
- 15 coriander leaves
- 150g of cherry tomatoes
- ¼ red onion
- 2 limes
- Salt and black pepper

Utensils:

* A knife
* A chopping board
* A bowl
* A serving platter
* A fork

1. *Peel the avocados and mash them in the bowl with a fork.*
2. *Chop the tomatoes into small pieces and add them to the avocados. Do the same with the red onion and coriander.*
3. *Mix all the ingredients together and squeeze the limes into the mixture.*

Little chef tips:

You can add as much coriander as you like and rip it up with your fingers instead of using a knife. Take out the tomato seeds to get a smoother texture.

"Edouard is a big fan of guacamole and loves having it for his breakfast with carrot sticks"

Tapenade

Ingredients (4 servings):

- 250g of black olives
- 8 basil leaves
- 1 anchovy
- 2 tablespoons of olive oil
- ½ garlic clove

Utensils:

* A blender

* A serving bowl

1. *Put the olives into the blender with the anchovy fillet, the garlic and the basil leaves. Blend until you get a smooth texture.*

2. *Slowly, pour in the olive oil until you get a smooth mixture.*

Little chef tips:

Eat it with some toast or croutons.

"I love eating tapenade with white fish and fennel seeds"

Hummus

Ingredients (4 servings):

- 2 cans of chickpeas
- 1 tablespoon of tahini paste
- 4 tablespoons of olive oil
- 1 teaspoon of cumin
- ½ lemon juice
- Salt and black pepper

Utensils:

* A knife
* A blender
* A bowl

1. *Rinse the chickpeas before putting them in the blender.*
2. *With the help of an adult, put all the ingredients in the blender.*
3. *Blend and pour in the olive oil intermittently.*

Little chef tips:

Swap the cumin for some paprika powder if you want to get new flavours.

"Like the guacamole, Edouard can eat hummus every day!"

Tomato sauce

Ingredients (4 servings):

- 2 cans of organic tomatoes
- 1 carrot
- ½ fennel bulb
- ½ aubergine
- 10 basil leaves
- 2 tablespoons of herbs de Provence
- Salt and black pepper
- 1 teaspoon of granulated sugar
- 1 tablespoon of olive oil

Utensils:

* A knife
* A chopping board
* A peeler
* A saucepan
* A wooden spoon
* A blender

1. *Pour the tomatoes into the saucepan and heat on a low temperature.*
2. *Peel and slice the carrot, the aubergine, the fennel and the basil leaves. Add them to the tomato sauce.*
3. *Sprinkle the herbs de Provence, salt, black pepper and sugar. Stir slowly and let it cook for 2 hours. Add some water if the sauce is a little bit too thick.*
4. *When all the vegetables are soft, blend your tomato sauce.*

Little chef tips:

You can add any vegetables but don't forget that courgettes are watery so the texture could be different if you add too much.

"It always brings me back to South of France when I cook it"

Preparation time: 5 minutes each

Vegan
Gluten Free

Salad dressings

Ingredients (4 servings):

- 2 tablespoons of olive oil
- 1 tablespoon of balsamic vinegar
- 1 teaspoon Dijon mustard
- Salt and black pepper

Utensils:

* A bowl
* A spoon

Ingredients (4 servings):

- 1 lemon
- 1 lime
- 1 teaspoon mango puree
- 10 coriander leaves
- Salt and black pepper

Utensils:

* A bowl
* A spoon

Ingredients (4 servings):

- 2 tablespoons olive oil
- 1 tablespoon soya sauce
- Sesame seeds (white or black)

Utensils:

* A bowl
* A spoon

Preparation time: 15 minutes
Cooking time: 20 minutes

Puff pastry

Ingredients (4 servings):

- 200g organic plain flour
- 80g soft butter, cut into pieces
- 1 teaspoon salt
- 1 teaspoon olive oil
- 100ml water

Utensils:

* A bowl
* A scale

1. *Put the flour into a bowl with the diced and soft butter.*
2. *Rub together with your hands to resemble breadcrumbs.*
3. *Add the salt, olive oil and pour the water.*
4. *Make a soft dough.*

Little chef tips:

Wrap your dough in cling film and chill for one hour.

Preparation time: 15 minutes
Cooking time: 10 minutes

Flatbread

Ingredients (6 flatbreads):

- 250g Greek yogurt
- 150g organic plain flour
- 2 teaspoons baking powder
- 50g melted butter
- Coriander, salt

Utensils:

* A bowl
* A frying pan
* A pastry brush
* A rolling pin
* A scale

1. *In a bowl, mix the dry ingredients together and combine with the yogurt.*
2. *Make a soft dough with your hands and knead for 2 minutes.*
3. *Dust a clean work surface with flour and divide your dough into 6 pieces.*
4. *Flatten them with a rolling pin.*
5. *Get the butter melted and chop some coriander leaves on it.*
6. *Turn on your cooker (on medium heat 5/6) and grease the frying pan.*
7. *Cook the bread. When it is cooked, flip it to cook the other side and brush all over with the melted butter and coriander.*

Little chef tips:

Add some cumin seeds to your dough to discover a new flavour.

Preparation time: 15 minutes

Crumble

Ingredients (4 servings):

- 150g organic plain flour
- 70g granulated sugar
- 80g organic unsalted soft butter

Utensils:

*A big bowl

* A scale

1. *In the bowl, put the flour and the sugar. Mix with your hands.*
2. *Add the butter and rub until your get a nice and light breadcrumb texture.*

Little chef tips:

Do not overwork, otherwise your crumble will become heavy.

Add 2 teaspoons of cinnamon when you make an apple or pear crumble.

"I always have a jar of crumble mixture in my fridge, in case I want to eat a fruity crumble"

Preparation time: 5 minutes

Flavoursome sugar

Cinnamon sugar:

- 300g granulated sugar
- 1 teaspoon cinnamon, ground
- *"My favourite one"*

Utensils:

* A bowl
* A spoon
* A scale

Vanilla sugar

- 300g coconut sugar
- 3 vanilla sticks, grated

Utensils:

* A bowl
* A spoon
* A scale

Christmas sugar:

- 300g brown sugar
- 1 teaspoon ginger, ground
- 2 teaspoons cinnamon, ground
- 2 teaspoons nutmeg, ground
- 1 teaspoon paprika

Utensils:

* A bowl
* A spoon
* A scale

Chocolate sugar:

- 300g coconut sugar
- 2 teaspoons cocoa powder
- 1 vanilla stick, grated

Utensils:

* A bowl
* A spoon
* A scale

THANK YOU

This book has been a wonderful chapter in my life and I am glad to share with you my recipes and the stories behind them.

Some families have believed in me since the beginning and supported me at different stages of Kids En Cuisine's evolution. A big thank you to Chloe, Pierre, Eliza who have been the first égéries of Kids En Cuisine. I am pretty sure you have already seen their faces on my website, on social media and in magazines.

Some little chefs have been cooking with me for years, learning many recipes along the way, and I have had the pleasure of seeing them growing up. A big thank you to Ines, Phoenix, Lia, Rocco, Ava and their families who hosted the weekly cooking classes.

You perhaps don't know, but Chef Teddy, who became the mascot of Kids En Cuisine and has reassured plenty of Mini Chefs during my classes, was given to me by a family who come to London once a year. Every year, they come during the winter and it's a joy to see how they've grown up and it means a lot that they are still enjoying the cooking classes with me. The coconut ball recipe was created for them a few years ago and it went on to become one of the most popular recipes of all time for Kids En Cuisine.

Isabella and Cecilia were great little models for this book and thanks also to their mums who were so helpful during the photoshoot.

Julia C has been one of the most helpful and supportive people during the whole process of this book. She has always been here to listen to me and seeing in me the capacity of finding the right balance between my son, Kids En Cuisine and this book.

Najla, for always being positive and encouraging me at any time.

Phil Hatcher, who used his skills as an English tutor and a photographer to do an amazing job of proofreading and taking the lovely photos of my son and me for the cover of this book.

Edouard, my son, who has been my source of inspiration since he was born with his taste for food already well developed. My little boy, I am still hoping to find a way to share with you the taste of cabbages, courgettes and dishes with sauces...

I hope you have a lovely time cooking my recipes with your little chefs and do not hesitate to share these yummy time with me.

Bon Appétit
Flo